Still With Me

Healing After Loss Of A Pet

By Elara Sage

Still With Me: Healing After Loss Of A Pet

ISBN: 978-81-992826-6-7 (paperback)

ISBN: 978-81-992826-0-5 (hardcover)

ISBN: 978-81-992826-5-0 (ebook)

Published by Seven Hues Books.

www.sevenhuesbooks.com

First edition, 2025.

Table of Contents

To Bruno,

My dearest companion, thank you for every tail wag, every wet-nosed nudge, and for filling my life with unconditional love. This is for you, my good boy. You are forever in my heart.

To Anyone Who's Ever Loved and Lost

If you're holding this book, it probably means your heart is hurting. Maybe you're in the early days of saying goodbye to a beloved pet. Maybe you've been carrying that grief for months, or years, and no one around you quite understands. Maybe you're just searching for a way to *breathe* through the ache.

I wrote this book for you. Whether your loss is fresh or decades old, whether you're an adult carrying silent grief or a parent supporting a child through their first goodbye, these pages are here to offer comfort and understanding.

As someone who has loved and lost animal companions, I know how deep the bond can go, and how quiet the world feels when they're gone. Pets are not "just" anything. They are family. They are our softest routines and our fiercest protectors. They make us laugh, teach us presence, and show us unconditional love. So, when they die, the grief is real. It is legitimate. And it deserves to be honored.

This book is a companion, not a prescription. It won't tell you how to grieve or when to move on. Instead, it will walk beside you through the messy, nonlinear, sacred journey of pet loss. You'll find practical support, emotional validation, and comforting words — some from the voice of the grieving human, and others imagined from the voice of the pet who's passed. Those letters are meant to feel like a whisper of comfort from the one you loved so much.

Each chapter offers space to reflect, remember, and reconnect with your pet, with yourself, and with life beyond your grief. You'll also find journal prompts, creative activities, gentle checklists, and poems designed to help you express what words alone can't always say.

When I lost my dog, there were days I could barely breathe without the sound of his paws padding behind me. I searched for his familiar presence in every room and was startled, again and again, by the absence. I kept his collar on the dresser, and his leash on the hook for weeks. And then, slowly, I started to find comfort in small rituals: lighting a candle in his memory, writing him letters, even speaking to him out loud. Grief didn't vanish, but it softened. And I realized I could carry both the pain and the love.

This book was born from those quiet moments, from the understanding that what we need is not a map to escape grief, but a companion who will sit beside us in it. I hope that these pages will do just that.

Above all, this book is a soft place to land. A keepsake for your grief. A reminder that you're not alone, and that healing is not about forgetting, it's about finding new ways to carry the love forward.

Thank you for trusting me to be part of your healing. Your grief matters. And so does the love that caused it.

With compassion,

— *Elara Sage*

Understanding the Bond: Why Pet Loss Hurts So Deeply

A tail that once thumped against the floor with joy is now still. The absence is sharp, not just in the routines, but in the rhythm of your heart. Maybe someone has told you, "It was just a dog," or "You can get another cat," but those words only deepen the ache. Because it wasn't just a dog. It wasn't just a cat. It was family! You are carrying the weight of a loss that the world doesn't fully understand, and may not even acknowledge.

It often begins with something small. An old collar found at the back of a drawer. The rustle of a food bag. The familiar time of day when the quiet click of paws would tap across the floor. And then comes the ache — a wave of grief that seems far too large for such a "simple" trigger.

But there is nothing simple about the relationship we share with our pets. The bond is deep, real, and profoundly emotional. For many, especially those who live alone, have faced trauma, or rely on their pet for daily emotional support, that bond can feel even deeper, sometimes becoming their most constant and trusted connection. It is built not just on routine, but on love, trust, comfort, and shared life. That's why their loss can shake us to our very core.

This chapter is about understanding that bond, not just from the heart, but also from the mind. To see why it hurts, we must first see why it mattered.

The Science of Attachment

Humans are wired for connection. From infancy, we form attachments to caregivers, companions, and those who bring us emotional safety. Pets, with their presence, affection, and routine, easily step into this role.

Modern neuroscience offers clarity about why the grief of pet loss feels so overwhelming. For many, understanding the science behind these bonds can be a relief. It shows that what you're feeling isn't an overreaction, but a natural, human response to losing a beloved companion. Research shows that the brain responds to our pets much like it does to human loved ones. Oxytocin, the "bonding hormone," is released when we pet our animals or even make eye contact. This hormone deepens attachment and reduces stress.

This same hormone helps parents bond with infants and helps couples to feel connected. Simply stroking a dog, cuddling a cat, or even watching a fish swim can lower cortisol (the stress hormone), while boosting serotonin and dopamine, which enhance mood.

This neurological dance happens every day in small moments: during belly rubs, shared naps, and evening walks. Over time, pets become woven into our neurobiological fabric. They regulate our emotions. They help us cope with loneliness, anxiety, and even trauma.

For many, the companionship of a pet provides the deepest form of emotional security, especially for those who live alone, experience social anxiety, or have gone through trauma. Pets become emotional anchors — the one constant in a sea of change.

So, when we lose them, we are not "just" losing a dog, a cat, or a bird. We're losing a regulated emotional system. A rhythm. A safe place. Our nervous system doesn't just miss them. It has to relearn how to function without that familiar source of calm and connection.

Additionally, the caregiving role we play in our pets' lives enhances attachment. We are their world. We choose their food, schedule their vet visits, and anticipate their needs. That sense of responsibility forms a powerful emotional loop, and it explains why their absence can feel like more than loss. It can feel as though a part of our identity has been stripped away.

Why This Loss Feels Different

Grief over pet loss is often intensified by the unique nature of the relationship we have with them. The bond we have with our pets is one of the purest forms of connection we experience, defined by simplicity and trust.

Unlike many human connections, the love we receive from pets is free from judgment, conditions, or complexity. Our pets witness our lives intimately; they see us at our best and worst and stay beside us anyway. They don't need us to explain ourselves, to justify our moods, or to hide our flaws.

Your dog never held a grudge. Your cat never asked you to explain yourself. Your rabbit didn't care what kind of day you'd had. They simply **loved**.

Their presence offers something increasingly rare in our fast-paced, performance-driven world: **unconditional companionship.**

This kind of acceptance is rare, and deeply healing. When it's gone, it leaves a unique void.

You may feel:

- A sense of disbelief or disorientation
- Guilt over decisions made
- Regret over things left unsaid or undone
- A heavy silence in your home
- Loneliness that cuts deeper than expected

All of these are normal.

A Shared Lifetime

For many of us, pets are an integral part of our home's identity. They are:

- The one who greeted us first
- The one who stayed near during the heartbreak
- The one who was always excited, no matter the day

What's often underestimated is the sheer amount of life we live *with* our pets.

They've been there through heartbreaks, moves, illnesses, career changes, and all the moments in between. They watched us grow. They kept our secrets. They were the warm spot at the foot of the bed, the soft sigh beside us during tough nights, the joyful chaos that made a bad day bearable.

They are caretakers, confidants, comic relief, exercise partners, and sleeping companions. For children, they are best friends. For elders, sometimes the only daily touchpoint.

They are there for every ordinary moment, which is why their absence affects us in extraordinary ways. They're not just part of our major life events; they're the quiet presence in between.

Their death removes more than a being; it changes the entire dynamic of the household. The rituals shift. The energy drops. The sense of 'home' feels altered.

We often say pets love us unconditionally. But what's less said is this: **we loved them with equal depth.** The grief is a measure of that love.

When Others Don't Understand

When a person we love dies, some rituals help us grieve: funerals, memorials, obituaries, and communal mourning. But when a pet dies, those rituals are often absent or minimized. We might quietly take a day off work, or we may be expected to carry on as if nothing happened. The world doesn't pause for pet grief. While a few workplaces and communities are starting to recognize the need for pet bereavement leave, for many, this support is still rare.

This cultural gap leaves many feeling isolated in their mourning. Yet the grief is no less real. In fact, it's often more complicated because it's invisible to others. Pet loss can be disenfranchised grief, the kind that isn't fully recognized or validated by society, even though it's as deep and consuming as any other form of loss.

It is one of the hardest aspects of grieving a pet, the lack of social acknowledgement. You may hear well-meaning but hurtful phrases like:

- *"It was just a dog."*
- *"You can get another one."*
- *"At least it wasn't a person."*

These comments dismiss the depth of your loss. They imply there's a hierarchy to grief — that human losses somehow count more. But grief isn't logical. It's relational. The amount you grieve for someone is directly related to the role they played in your life, not their species.

A Letter From Your Pet #1

Dear Human,

You loved me so well. I felt it in every meal you made, every walk you took me on, every time you let me curl up beside you. I know my absence hurts, because our bond was real.

But know this: I didn't leave with sadness in my heart. I left full of memories. Full of you. Every cuddle. Every silly nickname. Every quiet moment.

You were my whole world. And I was part of yours. That's why it hurts. And that's why your grief is valid.

Please don't rush your healing. I'm still with you, in every soft moment, in every tender thought. You gave me a beautiful life.

Now give yourself time to breathe through the ache of saying goodbye.

Love always,

Your grateful companion 🐾

Reflection Prompt: The First Hello

Let's go back to the beginning.

- Where did you first meet your pet?
- What drew you to them?
- What did you feel in those early days — excitement, nerves, instant connection?

Write about those first few days together (What you noticed, how you felt, and how you began to bond). How did your pet settle into your life? How did you settle into theirs?

"You were the smallest one in the litter. But you walked right up to me and wouldn't stop licking my shoe. That's when I knew you had picked me."

A Letter From Your Pet #2

Dear Human,

I knew the sound of your footsteps before you entered the room. I knew your scent, your moods, and the rhythm of your days. I was your shadow, your warmth on cold nights, your quiet joy in the middle of long, hard days.

Now, I see you reaching for me and stopping short. I see your eyes linger on my empty bed, your breath caught when a memory sneaks up out of nowhere. I want you to know, I felt every ounce of your love. It lived in your hands when you scratched behind my ears. In your voice when you whispered silly things. In your quiet presence when you just sat beside me.

I didn't leave because I stopped loving you. I left because my time was done, and I trusted you to let me go. But I'm still here. In the morning light. In the silence we used to share. In the heartbeat that still remembers mine.

Thank you for being my person.

With all my love,

Your forever friend

Reflection Prompt: What Made Our Bond Special?

Take a few moments to write about what made your relationship unique:

- What did your pet know about you that no one else did?
- When did you feel most connected?
- What were your unspoken rituals?
- What do you miss most right now?

"She always waited by the door when I got home, no matter what time it was. I didn't realize how much I needed that until it was gone."

A Letter From Your Pet #3

Dear Human,

You used to laugh when I chased shadows, barked at nothing, or fell asleep mid-chew. You didn't care that I snored or shed everywhere. You just loved me. That was enough.

I want you to know something: I loved my life. Even the simple parts, waiting at the door, licking peanut butter from a spoon, listening to your favorite song on loop. You made everything feel like home.

I wasn't afraid when I left. I just felt tired, and then I felt light. You don't have to be strong all the time. It's okay to cry. But please don't carry guilt, it has no place between us. Only love does. And love never ends.

Still watching over you,

Your faithful friend 🐾

Journal Prompt: "What You Taught Me"

Complete these sentences in your journal:

- "You taught me to…"
- "I'll never forget the time we…"
- "Because of you, I now understand…"

The lessons we learn from our pets are often quiet ones — patience, presence, joy in the mundane. Honor those lessons by naming them.

Closing Poem

"Why It Hurts"

You weren't my whole life,
But you filled every quiet space.
A tail, a look, a morning stretch,
A gentle, furry grace.

You asked for little, gave so much,
And asked for nothing more
Than just to sit beside my feet,
To greet me at the door.

Now silence fills those corners,
But love still finds its way.
In memories, in tears, in light
You're with me every day.

Love doesn't end when a heartbeat stops. It shifts forms, from fur to memory, from presence to legacy. That bond? It's still here. So, let's begin this journey together, not to forget, but to remember with grace.

The Grief Journey: What to Expect When Your Pet Dies

Grief has a way of ambushing us. It doesn't always begin the moment we say goodbye. It can begin before that, in the quiet dread of knowing the end is near. And it doesn't end when the ashes are returned or the bed is packed away. It lingers in the smallest places: the sound of the door that no longer brings running paws, the space on the couch, even the habit of speaking aloud to someone who is no longer there.

When a beloved pet dies, you don't just lose a companion, you lose part of your identity, your routine, and your emotional foundation. The grief can be just as sharp, and sometimes sharper, than when we lose a human. Yet, this truth is often dismissed. People may not understand. You may feel pressure to "move on." But the reality is: your grief is valid. It is a testament to love. And love, in any form, deserves to be grieved.

The Nature of Pet Grief

Pet grief is real grief. This isn't a watered-down version of human loss, it's its own kind of deep, aching absence. It can be even more painful because of how entwined pets become with our everyday lives. They don't just witness our routines, they shape them. They wake us up, greet us at the door, and follow us from room to room. They're silent companions through heartbreak, illness, and joy. Losing them isn't just losing someone you love. It's losing the rhythm of your days.

And then comes the added wound: the minimization of that grief by others. You may hear, "It was just a pet," or "You can get another one." These comments, however well-meaning, only deepen your pain. Grief that goes unrecognized is especially difficult to bear. This is known as disenfranchised grief — grief that isn't openly acknowledged or socially supported. It leaves you feeling alone just when you need connection the most.

But make no mistake: your grief is real, and it deserves space. You are allowed to mourn deeply. You are allowed to break down. You are allowed to take your time.

How Pet Grief Mirrors Human Grief

You may find yourself surprised at just how *human* your grief feels. The emotional turmoil, the daily heartbreak, even the physical symptoms. These are not unlike the grief experienced when a person dies. That's because your brain does not differentiate based on species. It responds to *loss*, and the deeper the love, the more profound the pain.

Research in bereavement psychology shows that losing a pet can trigger the same biochemical stress responses as losing a close family member. Yet many people feel ashamed or invalidated for grieving "too much." This silence around pet grief can create a secondary layer of emotional pain, what's often called "disenfranchised grief."

Naming your grief helps heal it. This isn't an overreaction. It's a testament to the bond you built.

The Emotional Landscape: What Grief Can Look Like

Grief doesn't move in a straight line. It doesn't arrive in predictable stages and leave in a tidy fashion. It's messy, cyclical, and unique to every person. Some days, it feels like a tightness in your chest or a lump in your throat. Other days, it feels like exhaustion that makes even small tasks impossible. Still, some common emotional responses may help you recognize your own experience:

Denial

"I keep expecting to hear her nails clicking on the floor."

Denial is a form of emotional anesthesia. It protects us from feeling the full weight of the loss all at once. You may go through the motions in a daze, forgetting they're gone for a moment and then remembering with a fresh wave of pain.

Anger

"Why did this happen? Why so soon? Why couldn't I do more?"

Anger can arise at others, at yourself, or even at your pet for leaving. It's okay. Anger is part of the grieving process, and beneath it is often a deep well of sadness and helplessness.

Bargaining

"If I had taken her to the vet sooner…"

We play out different scenarios in our minds, trying to rewrite the story. This is a way of trying to make sense of loss, of finding some sense of control in a moment where everything feels broken.

Depression

"I can't stop crying. Nothing feels right without him."

This is the hollow part, the heaviness that settles into your bones. You may feel numb, exhausted, or disinterested in things you usually enjoy. This phase, though dark, is part of the natural grief process. It doesn't mean you're broken. It means you're mourning.

Acceptance

"I'll always miss her, but I can smile when I think of her now."

Acceptance doesn't mean you're "over it." It means you've begun to live with the loss instead of constantly fighting it. You can carry the pain and the love together.

These aren't steps you pass through once. You may revisit them over and over. For some, grief doesn't fully arrive until weeks or months later, when the routines have shifted and the quiet moments settle in. One moment, you're okay. Next, you're crying in the grocery store because you passed the pet food aisle. This is normal. This is grief. And if you don't experience all these feelings, or if they come in a different order, that's okay too.

Complex Emotions You Might Feel

Guilt

This is perhaps the most common and complicated feeling after pet loss.

"Did I wait too long to say goodbye?" "Did I give them a good enough life?" "Was it really time?"

Especially in cases involving euthanasia, guilt can be overwhelming. But guilt often masks love. It means you cared so deeply, you wanted their life to be perfect. No decision is ever easy. But if you chose with compassion, you chose well.

Relief

This emotion can feel shameful, but it's also normal. If your pet suffered in the end, part of you may feel relieved that they're no longer in pain. This doesn't mean you didn't love them. It means you loved them enough to want their suffering to end.

Isolation

Even well-meaning people might not get it. They might compare it to other forms of loss or suggest you should "move on." This can make you feel alone in your pain. Seeking out others who understand can make a huge difference.

Numbness

You may feel nothing for a while. No tears, no strong emotions, just blankness. This, too, is part of grief. It's your mind's way of coping when the heart is too overwhelmed.

Physical Symptoms of Grief

Grief isn't just emotional; it lives in the body. You might experience:

- Fatigue and exhaustion
- Sleep disturbances
- Appetite changes
- Aches and tension
- Crying spells
- Trouble concentrating
- Anxiety or chest tightness

Some people even experience "phantom" sensations, hearing a bark, feeling a nudge, glimpsing their pet's shape out of the corner of their eye. These moments can be both comforting and painful. You're not imagining things. You're remembering with your whole body. These sensations are your mind and body trying to process what's missing. They are common, and they will soften over time.

What Helps

There is no shortcut through grief. But some tools can help you move through it with compassion:

- **Give yourself permission to feel.** Don't judge your emotions. Name them, sit with them, and let them move through you.
- **Talk to someone.** Whether it's a friend, therapist, or pet loss support group, sharing your experience can help you feel less alone.
- **Create small rituals.** Light a candle. Write a letter. Say their name aloud. Rituals create space for grief to breathe.
- **Journal your feelings.** Sometimes words on paper can offer clarity and calm.

- **Be gentle with yourself.** Lower your expectations. Rest. Nourish your body. It's okay not to function at 100%.

When Grief Doesn't Follow the Stages

We discussed the five stages of grief: denial, anger, bargaining, depression, and acceptance. While this model can help name your feelings, it was never meant to be a step-by-step instruction manual.

You might feel acceptance one day, then fall back into anger the next. Or experience joy recalling a memory, only to be hit by despair moments later. This is normal. Grief moves in a spiral, not a straight line. It revisits itself, loops, contracts, and expands.

Try not to measure your healing by how long it's been since the loss. Instead, look for tiny signs of self-compassion. Did you eat today? Did you take a walk? Did you remember something without crying? That's progress.

A Letter From Your Pet #4

Dear Human,

I see your tears. I feel the ache in your heart. I know you replay my last day over and over again. But please, don't let the ending become the whole story.

I remember the walks. The naps. The treats you snuck me when no one was looking. I remember the way you spoke my name like it was sacred. I remember love, every single day.

You gave me a beautiful life. You gave me safety. You gave me your heart.

And now, I give you this: permission to grieve, to rest, to smile again when you're ready. I'm not gone, I've just slipped into the quiet parts of your soul.

When you laugh again, I'll be there. When you love again, I'll be there.

Always.
Yours still,

Your grateful shadow 🐾

Reflection Prompt: "When Did It Feel Real?"

Take a moment to reflect on the days after your pet's passing.

- Was there a specific moment it hit you—really hit you—that they were gone?
- What triggered that feeling? A quiet morning? An empty bowl?
- What did you do, think, or feel at that moment?

Writing this down might bring up pain, but it also helps you process. The truth already lives in your heart. Giving it words can bring release. If you feel nothing as you write, that's normal too. Numbness is one way your heart protects itself.

"It hit me when I woke up and didn't hear her snoring beside me. That silence wasn't peaceful. It felt deafening."

Grief Checklist: Have You Felt…

- Guilt about how it happened or ended
- Sudden crying spells or emotional outbursts
- Feeling like you "should be over it" by now
- Difficulty sleeping or eating
- Wanting to talk about your pet, but not knowing who to talk to
- Feeling relief, and then guilt for that relief
- Dreaming about your pet
- Feeling like they're still near
- Avoiding places or things that remind you of them

If you checked more than one, you are not alone. These are normal parts of grieving. There is no timeline. Your heart is doing its best to mend.

Personal Story: Max and the Morning Coffee

Lena lost her dog Max after 12 years together. “I thought I was ready,” she said. “He had been declining. I had made peace with it, or so I thought.”

But the day after Max passed, Lena poured two cups of coffee. She always poured one for herself and one in Max’s bowl—he loved a splash of milk. She stood in the kitchen, staring at the second cup, her hands shaking.

“That’s when it hit me,” she said. “He was really gone.”

She cried, then she laughed, because Max would have found the spilt coffee hilarious. Now, she pours that second cup once a week, just for him.

“It sounds silly,” Lena says, “but it makes me feel like he’s still part of my mornings. And maybe he is.”

Closing Poem

"Waves"

Grief doesn't ask permission,
It rolls in like a tide,
Washing away the ordinary,
Leaving only ache and memory.

But then, a sunrise,
A gentle breeze,
A sudden laugh,
And for a moment, you breathe.

This is how it comes,
Not in a straight line,
But in waves.
And one day, those waves won't knock you over.
They'll carry you instead.

Grief is not something to get over. It's something you learn to live with, to honor, to move through. There is no right way. There is only your way.

And whatever that looks like — it's enough.

When the Rainbow Bridge Feels Too Far: Coping with Overwhelming Grief

In the hours and days after your pet's passing, everything can feel surreal. You might forget for a moment and call their name. You might reach out to feed them or check their bed, only to remember again. That dull ache in your chest? That's not your imagination. It's grief. It settles into the body, dull and heavy, or sharp and sudden, taking your breath away.

This chapter is for those moments, the ones that feel too big to survive. Getting out of bed seems impossible. When your whole being aches for a presence that is no longer there. If you've ever whispered, "I can't do this," then this page is for you.

Acute Grief: The First Shock

Acute grief is the body's emergency response to deep emotional pain. It's why you might feel like you're moving in slow motion, why you forget simple things, or why you suddenly burst into tears doing something as mundane as opening the fridge. Your system is overwhelmed. And it's okay.

Some people experience nausea, panic attacks, or exhaustion. Others go numb, unable to cry at all. Both are valid. Grief doesn't come in a predictable form. There is no script, no standard.

What matters most in this stage is simply this: survival. Not thriving. Not bouncing back. Just getting through the next breath, the next hour, the next day.

When Grief Feels Like Panic

There's a certain kind of grief that doesn't just ache, it floods. Your heart races, your chest tightens, and you might feel like you're drowning in emotion. This is acute grief, and it often comes in waves. It can be especially intense after losing a pet who was part of your daily rhythm. The quiet becomes deafening. The routines feel hollow.

In these moments, your body doesn't just miss your pet, it reacts as if part of your identity has been ripped away. That's because, in a very real sense, it has. You didn't just lose a companion, you lost your emotional anchor, your walking buddy, your morning greeting.

Emotional First Aid

Just like physical wounds need tending, emotional wounds do too. Here are a few tools that can help during intense grief episodes:

1. The 5-4-3-2-1 Grounding Technique

- 5 things you can see
- 4 things you can touch
- 3 things you can hear
- 2 things you can smell
- 1 thing you can taste

This technique pulls your mind back from spiraling thoughts and brings you into the safety of the present moment.

2. Breathe with Intention

Inhale deeply through your nose for 4 counts, hold for 4 counts, and exhale slowly through your mouth for 6 counts. Repeat. You are reminding your body that it is safe, even if your heart doesn't feel it yet.

3. Crying Is Not Weakness

Tears release stress hormones and activate the parasympathetic nervous system (the one responsible for calming you). Let yourself cry. It's not a failure, it's a release.

4. Touch Memory Objects:

Hold your pet's tag, a photo, or a toy. Let the memory flow through you like warmth, not pain.

5. Grief Breaks

Set a timer for 20 minutes to allow yourself to fully grieve. Then, take a break. Walk. Make tea. Stretch. You can always return to your grief. But it's okay to take small rests from the intensity.

6. Look at the Sky: Sometimes, just remembering the world is still turning helps you feel rooted.

You are not trying to escape the pain. You are learning how to hold it without being consumed by it.

Mindfulness and Gentle Distraction

You don't need to stay in the storm of grief every minute. Sometimes, the kindest thing you can do for yourself is to step away, even briefly.

- Fold laundry while listening to soft music.
- Watch a calming nature video.
- Doodle, color, or finger-paint.
- Make a simple meal.
- Sit in the sun and notice the warmth.

None of this erases your grief. But it gives your heart a breather. And that matters.

Permission to Break Down

Let's be clear: you are not expected to "keep it together." There is no prize for stoicism in the face of loss. You don't have to be strong. You don't have to make sense. You don't have to explain your tears.

Breaking down is often part of the healing. Think of it not as falling apart, but as allowing the weight of love to move through you in all its rawness.

"How Long Will This Hurt?"

This is the question many grieving pet parents ask. And the honest answer is: it hurts as long as it needs to.

Grief does not follow a calendar. You may feel numb one day, shattered the next, then calm for a stretch, only to dissolve at the sight of an old toy under the couch.

The pain softens. It changes. You will not feel this way forever. But you will carry the love, and yes, the ache, in some form, always.

That's not a burden. It's a bond.

What to Do When You Can't Sleep

Nights can be especially brutal after a loss. The silence is louder. The bed feels bigger. The shadows are longer. If sleep becomes elusive, consider gentle rituals:

- Light a candle in your pet's memory
- Write a short letter or journal entry
- Play soft instrumental music or white noise
- Keep a "grief box" beside your bed with comfort items (a soft blanket, their tag, photos)
- Try a visualization: Picture your pet curled up beside you, keeping watch, safe and content

Insomnia during grief is normal. But it's okay to let your body rest even if you don't sleep. Just allowing your body to be still can be a form of healing.

A Letter For the Days That Feel Too Heavy

Dear Human,

I know you're hurting. I see you in the dark, hand pressed against my collar. I hear the silence in the spaces we used to fill together. And I wish I could sit beside you again, just to nudge your hand and remind you that you're not alone.

I didn't want to leave you. But I want you to know this: I felt your love in every moment. In your voice. Your touch. The way you stayed with me, even when it was hard.

Please don't be angry at yourself. You did everything right. Even when it hurts. Even when it broke your heart.

When you ache, I ache with you. But when you remember the good times, those sunlit walks, the way we danced in the kitchen. I feel that joy too.

I'm still nearby. In the soft wind. The warm patch of sunlight. The quiet moments when you suddenly feel me close.

You gave me a beautiful life. Let that be your comfort. And when the pain softens, I'll still be walking with you, just in a different way.

Always,
Your little shadow 🐾

When You Feel Like You're Going Backwards

Many people feel a return of grief weeks or months after they thought they were "doing better." This is not failure. This is how grief works. It can be triggered by holidays, smells, routines, or random memories.

These backwards steps are part of the forward movement.

Think of grief like the tide. It rushes in, sometimes unexpectedly. But it also recedes, quietly, gently. The key is not to fight the waves, but to find a way to float.

Reflection Prompt: Describe What Today Felt Like

Take five minutes. No filter, no need for grammar or structure. Just let the pen move.

- How did grief show up today?
- What helped you cope, even for a moment?

- What memory rose?

"Today I stayed in bed too long. I smelled their blanket and cried. Then I sat outside for a few minutes. I think they would've liked that."

A Whisper – In Your Hardest Moment

Dear Human,

I saw you on the floor today. The world had stopped for you, hadn't it? You clutched my leash, or my blanket, or maybe just your heart, and everything hurt.

I wanted to curl up beside you. To press my nose against your cheek. I wanted to do all the things I used to do to make you feel okay.

But instead, I whispered through the breeze. I laid a moment of stillness across your shoulders. I curled around you in the way only memory can.

You are not broken. You are grieving. That means we mattered. That means you loved deeply and fully.

So please, cry if you need to. Yell if you must. But don't forget this: I would choose you again, every single time.

Love always,

Your shadow, your tail, your forever friend 🐾

What's Helping Right Now (Even a Little)

Check anything that feels even slightly comforting:

- Having a familiar routine (e.g., morning tea, walking the same path)
- Talking to a friend or writing in a journal
- Keeping a special item nearby (collar, photo, toy)
- Looking through old photos or videos
- Sitting in the sun or near a window
- Letting yourself cry
- Getting a full night of sleep
- Lighting a candle or saying their name
- Remembering that grief is love, continuing

Even one checkmark is enough. Even reading this list is an act of care.

Reflection Prompt: What Helps Me Breathe When It's Hard?

Take a moment to list or write through answers to these:

- Who can I talk to when the feelings feel too big?
- What spaces make me feel safe?
- What comfort object helps me feel connected to my pet?
- What words or phrases bring me calm?
- When was the last time I surprised myself with strength?

Closing Poem

"Still Here"

You think I've left, but I am near,
I live in love, not bound by time or year.
I rest in the corners of your days,
In silent glances, a softened gaze.

I'm in the sigh, the morning breeze,
The rustle in the swaying trees.
Though paws no longer pad the floor,
My heart walks with you ever more.

You don't have to be okay today. You only have to be honest. The Rainbow Bridge might feel too far now, but love, your love — is still here. And in time, that love will lead you gently forward.

Making Difficult Decisions: Navigating Guilt and Regret

If you're holding guilt right now, you're not alone. Guilt often shows up like a shadow in the days after loss. It whispers doubts. Replays moments. Revisits decisions. It's that haunting "what if" that follows you around the house:

What if I had done more? What if I had noticed sooner? What if I'd waited just one more day?

This chapter is a safe place for those questions. Not to silence them, but to soften them. Guilt is a natural part of love. When we love deeply, we take responsibility deeply. But the truth is: perfect endings are rare. Most of us are left with things we wish we could have changed. That doesn't mean we failed. It means we cared.

The Weight of Guilt

Grief is often complicated by guilt. And in pet loss, this is especially true. We are their caregivers. Their advocates. Their protectors. So, when they die, no matter how peaceful or traumatic, it's easy to feel that somehow, we've let them down.

You might wonder:

- *Did I wait too long to take them to the vet?*
- *Did I make the right choice with euthanasia?*
- *Were they scared?*
- *Was I selfish in wanting more time?*

These questions are rooted in love, not failure. You are grieving because you loved them so well. And loving deeply means you now carry the burden of wondering if you did enough.

But here's what you need to hear: you did your best with the knowledge and emotional capacity you had in that moment. And your best was rooted in love. That is always enough.

Euthanasia: A Mercy Wrapped in Pain

One of the most complex decisions a pet parent may face is euthanasia. It goes against our instincts to choose death, even when it's to end suffering. You may struggle with that decision for months or years afterwards.

You may wonder:

- *Did I choose too soon?*
- *Should I have waited for a "sign"?*

- *Did they want more time?*

But consider this: ending pain is the final act of love we can offer. Pets don't understand medical interventions or future hope. They live in the now. And when their "now" is pain, confusion, or fear, choosing peace is not giving up. It's letting go with compassion.

Most veterinarians agree: we tend to wait too long, not act too soon. Because we don't want to say goodbye. But our pets trust us to make that decision when their world becomes too small, too painful.

Forgive yourself for making that call. You did not end their life. You ended their suffering.

Letting Go of "I Should Have…"

Regret often speaks in the language of hindsight.

I should have noticed sooner. I should have given more attention. I should have taken them to the vet that one time. I should have gotten a second opinion.

But here's the truth: we do the best we can with the information and resources we have at the time. Every decision you made was from a place of love, even if it didn't turn out the way you hoped.

Try this reframe:

- Instead of "I should have done more," say, *"I loved with all I had."*
- Instead of "I didn't catch it early enough," say, *"I gave them safety every day they were here."*
- Instead of "I failed them," say, *"I walked beside them to the end."*

Sudden Death and the Shock of No Goodbye

Sometimes we don't get to make a choice. Sometimes a pet dies suddenly — in an accident, from an undetected illness, or during surgery. The grief in these cases carries an extra weight: the shock of no goodbye.

You might feel cheated. Haunted by your last interaction. Maybe you weren't there. Maybe the last moment was rushed, ordinary, or distracted.

These thoughts can stick: "I wasn't there for them." But pause. Ask yourself: Were you there for them through their life? Did you give them safety, comfort, and love? If so, you were there. Not in one final moment, but in every meaningful one.

Pets live in patterns of care. In the food you gave, the walks you took, the naps you shared. That's what they remember. That's what mattered.

The Myth of the "Perfect Goodbye"

There's no such thing as a perfect goodbye. Whether you were with your pet when they passed or not, whether you held them in your arms or they slipped away at home alone, the ending never feels tidy.

Many people carry pain from not being there in the final moment. Maybe they passed at the vet's office when you were in traffic. Maybe it was while you were asleep. Maybe you were out of town.

That doesn't make your love incomplete. Love is not defined by a single moment. It's all the time you shared: the care, the laughter, the comfort. It lives in the everyday, not just the end.

Understanding the Guilt-Grief Cycle

Grief and guilt often dance together. The brain seeks answers to explain pain, and sometimes guilt becomes a default mechanism: it gives a false sense of control. *If I had just done this differently,* we think, *maybe they'd still be here.*

But guilt doesn't change the past, it just clings to it. Healing begins when we allow ourselves to grieve *without punishing ourselves.* You are allowed to feel sorrow without self-blame.

Ask yourself: If your pet could speak right now, would they want you to carry guilt? Or would they want you to carry the love?

Guilt Is the Language of Love

What if we viewed guilt not as proof of failure, but as evidence of love? Guilt is the mind trying to solve what the heart cannot undo.

It shows up not because you did wrong, but because you wish you could have done more. That's empathy. That's loyalty. That's grief, in one of its most tender forms.

You are not guilty. You are grieving. And you are doing it with a heart that loves deeply.

Forgiving Yourself

Forgiveness isn't forgetting. It's gently untangling yourself from self-blame.

Try speaking these words aloud:

- *"I made the best choices I could with the knowledge I had."*

- *My love outweighed my mistakes."*
- *"I release myself from the burden of needing to be perfect."*
- *"They knew I loved them. That was always enough."*

Forgiveness is a practice. You may have to offer it to yourself again and again. That's okay. It's not about erasing pain, it's about walking with it more kindly.

A Letter From Your Pet – You Did Enough

Dear Human,

I know you're hurting. I see the questions in your eyes. I hear the things you wish you could take back. But let me tell you what I remember:

I remember your voice. The softness in it, even when you were tired. I remember the way your hands held me, always gentle, even when they trembled. I remember the way you made hard choices, even when they broke your heart.

You did not fail me. You freed me.

Please stop holding pain like punishment. I never asked that of you. Hold the love instead. That's what I carried with me.

I loved my life. I loved you. And I still do.

Yours always,

Your brave-hearted friend 🐾

Reflection Prompt: What Would You Say to Each Other?

Take a quiet moment to write freely.

- What do you wish you could say to your pet?
- What do you believe they would say in return?
- If guilt were love, what is it trying to protect?

"I'm sorry I couldn't be with you at the end. But you were with me through everything else. That's what I remember."

Goodbye Letter or Apology Exercise

Set a timer for 10 minutes. Begin with:

- *"I want you to know I tried…"*
- *"I wish I had known…"*
- *"Thank you for…"*
- *"Please forgive me for…"*

Then, finish with:

- *"You meant the world to me."*
- *"You were never 'just a pet.'"*

- *"I carry you in everything I do now."*

Keep this letter, burn it safely, or read it aloud. It's your ritual.

Did I Love My Pet? A Reframing Checklist

Sometimes guilt clouds the obvious. Ask yourself:

- Did I feed them, shelter them, protect them?
- Did I notice when they were sick, in pain, or afraid?
- Did I talk to them, even if they couldn't talk back?
- Did I learn what they liked? What made them happy?
- Did I try to make their life better in any way?
- Did I cry when they left?

If you checked any of these, you loved them. That love is enough.

Message From Your Pet – About the Day I Left

Dear Human,

I know that day lives in your heart like a bruise. You replay it over and over. You wonder if you should have waited… or acted sooner… or done something different.

But I need you to know this: ***I didn't measure your love by my final breath. I felt it every single day.***

I didn't fear the end because I trusted you. I still do. You gave me comfort when I was afraid. You gave me peace when I was tired. And you gave me dignity when my body could no longer keep up.

Please don't hold guilt in the space where gratitude belongs. You were my home. You were my safety. You were everything.

With love beyond the bridge,

Your grateful heart on four legs 🐾

Reflection Prompt: Rewriting My Inner Narrative

Choose one statement from below and finish it in your journal:

- "I acted with compassion when I…"
- "Even though I carry guilt, I also know that I…"
- "My pet would remind me of all the times I…"
- "One thing I'm learning to forgive in myself is…"

Closing Poem

"Enough"

You wonder if you did too little,
If you missed the signs, the sound, the sigh.
But love is not measured in moments,
It's the days you never said goodbye.

It's the walks, the meals, the quiet nights,
The way they knew your every mood.
It's how your love became their world,
How you gave, and gave, and stood.

You did enough. You loved enough.
Let that be the truth that stays.
You were their forever.
And they were yours, all their days.

Creating Meaningful Memorials: Honoring Your Pet's Legacy

When a beloved pet passes, we're left with more than silence; we're left with stories, memories, and a love that has nowhere to go. That love doesn't disappear. It lingers. It wants to be expressed. And one of the most healing things we can do is to give it a home: in a memorial, a ritual, a creation, or a sacred space.

Creating a tribute to your pet isn't about "moving on." It's about continuing. It's about finding new ways to connect to the bond that still lives inside you. When we honor the life they shared with us, we give our grief a voice, and that voice, over time, becomes softer, clearer, and filled with love.

Why Memorials Matter

Memorials don't need to be grand. They need to be **true**. True to your pet, your bond, your grief, and your way of expressing love. Whether it's a framed photo, a candlelit corner, or a written letter tucked in a drawer, what matters is the meaning behind it.

In grief, we often search for ways to stay connected. A memorial provides that bridge. It becomes a way to:

- Tell their story
- Keep their presence woven into daily life
- Provide structure for honoring anniversaries or emotional moments
- Turn pain into a quiet sense of peace

Memorials help us anchor our love. They remind us that our pet mattered. That they lived, they loved, and they were deeply loved in return.

Why Rituals Matter (Even if You Have to Create Your Own)

Rituals help us mark loss and give shape to pain. When you lose a pet, you might not get flowers or sympathy cards. But that doesn't mean you shouldn't create your acts of remembrance.

Consider:

- Lighting a candle

- Writing them letters when you miss them
- Creating a memory box with photos, collars, or toys
- Saying their name out loud
- Planting a tree or flower in their honor

Rituals give grief a space to land. They allow us to say: this mattered. ***You* mattered.**

Ways to Remember: Finding What Speaks to You

There's no single "right" way to honor your pet's memory. Below are options. Choose what feels natural or inspiring. You can combine several or create your own.

1. Physical Memorials

- **Shadow Box:** Include their collar, a favorite toy, photos, or a lock of fur
- **Photo Album or Scrapbook:** Chronicle their life from adoption to their final days
- **Personal Jewelry:** Paw print pendants, engraved tags, or cremation jewelry
- **Framed Paw Print or Nose Print:** Many vets offer these as keepsakes

- **Urn or Memorial Box:** Personalized containers for ashes or mementos

2. Living Memorials

- **Plant a Tree or Garden:** Choose a tree, bush, or flowers that remind you of your pet's personality
- **Adopt-a-Bench or Brick:** Some parks and shelters offer memorial engraving opportunities
- **Donate in Their Name:** Support an animal shelter, rescue group, or cause they'd "approve" of

3. Creative Tributes

- **Write a Poem, Letter, or Story:** Express what they meant to you
- **Paint or Sketch Their Portrait:** No artistic skill required. It's about connection
- **Create a Video:** A montage of clips and photos set to music they "liked"
- **Craft a Song or Playlist:** Music that reminds you of shared moments

4. Rituals and Ceremonies

- **Candlelight Tribute:** Light a candle each year on their adoption date or the day they passed

- **Home Ceremony:** Invite family or close friends to share memories and say goodbye
- **Release Ritual:** Scatter flower petals, plant seeds, or release floating lanterns in their honor

5. Digital Memorials

- **Online Tribute Page:** Many pet sites allow you to post stories, photos, and memories
- **Social Media Memorial:** A post, highlight reel, or dedicated page to their legacy
- **Shared Album:** Invite friends and family to upload photos and moments they shared with your pet

Telling Their Story: The Healing Power of Memory

Sometimes we remember our pets in fragments—a certain bark, a favorite spot on the couch, the way they tilted their head when we said "walk." Bringing those fragments together can be deeply healing.

Try sitting down and writing their story. Not just how they died, but how they lived.

- Where did you meet?

- What were their quirks?
- What did they love more than anything?
- What made them "them"?

Telling their story makes the love tangible. It allows you to carry them forward, not just as a loss, but as a legacy.

Shared Memory: Family, Friends, and Children

If you lived with others who loved your pet, spouse, roommates, or kids, memorializing together can be a shared step in healing.

Ideas for Group Tributes:

- **Create a "Book of Memories":** Everyone writes one favorite story, then binds them together
- **Host a Memory Night:** Share stories, light candles, pass around photos
- **Make a Memory Jar:** Fill it with slips of paper containing memories, quotes, or silly moments
- Have kids draw their favorite memory or write a letter to their pet

Grief looks different for everyone. Some might want to talk. Others won't. That's okay. Honor each person's way of mourning, and offer shared space for remembrance without pressure.

Memorializing Through Daily Rituals

Not all memorials are static objects or one-time ceremonies. Some of the most powerful tributes are the simple, **daily rituals** that reconnect us to the memory of our pet. These gestures don't require time or money; they just require presence.

Consider these examples:

- **Filling their water bowl each morning**, not because they'll drink from it, but because it reminds you of care.
- **Leaving a spot open on the couch or bed**, just as they liked it.
- **Touching their collar or photo** before you leave the house.
- **Carrying a favorite phrase or nickname into your daily speech.**

These small acts, repeated over time, create a new kind of companionship. A continued relationship built on memory. You're not "living in the past." You're honoring a love that shaped your life.

Some people even create a **ritual walk** — going on a short stroll at the same time they once did with their dog, or visiting a favorite tree or bench that held meaning. You might bring a flower or simply sit in silence.

Let the ordinary become sacred. This, too, is how healing begins.

A Letter From Your Pet – Thank You for Remembering

Dear Human,

I saw the candle you lit. I heard the song you played. I felt the way your heart held me, even when your arms could not.

Thank you for remembering me with love and not just sadness. Every flower you plant, every word you write, every photo you frame, tells the world: I was here. I mattered. I was loved.

You didn't forget me. You carried me forward.

That's the best tribute I could ever ask for.

And when you smile, remembering me, I'm there too.

Always,

Your forever companion 🐾

Reflection Prompt: What Do You Want the World to Know?

Finish the sentence:

"If I could tell the world one thing about my pet, it would be…"

Then take it a step further:

"Their legacy is…"

- The love they taught you
- The way they made you feel safe
- The joy they brought to others

Let their story echo through your words.

Memory Exercise: A Perfect Day Together

Close your eyes and imagine:

- It's a peaceful morning. Your pet is healthy, happy, and beside you.
- What do you do first? Where do you go? What do you eat? How do you play?

- What moments make you laugh?
- How do you end the day?

Write it out, or simply picture it. This exercise isn't about what was, but about what felt true.

It becomes a touchstone, a memory to visit when you miss them most.

Memorial Ideas Checklist

Check off anything that speaks to you:

- Create a framed photo collage
- Plant a tree or flower in their name
- Write a letter and keep it in a special place
- Make a donation to a shelter or rescue
- Craft a shadow box with their items
- Hold a small memorial ceremony
- Light a candle on special dates
- Start a "memory journal" to write down memories as they come
- Build or buy a small memorial stone for the garden

- Share their story online

You don't have to do everything. You don't have to do it today. Just choose what helps your heart feel connected.

Closing Poem

"In the Garden of Memory"

You planted love where paws had been,
And watered grief with gentle hands.
A flower bloomed — a sacred thing,
A place where memory softly stands.

No leash, no bowl, no chewed-up toy,
But there — a photo, and a light.
A heart once full, now bruised and brave,
Still beating, still holding tight.

You gave me roots. I gave you wings.
And now, in petals, peace still sings.

Memorials are not just about looking back. They're about carrying forward. You're not closing a chapter, you're writing a new one, with your pet's memory as part of every page.

Navigating Daily Life Without Your Companion

There's a quiet that comes after a pet dies. Not a peaceful silence, but a jarring absence. The sound of paws that no longer follow you from room to room. The click of a leash that no longer signals joy. The food bowl that stays full, untouched. These are the small echoes of a life shared, and now missing.

This chapter is about what happens next. Not the big milestones, but the ordinary hours: the morning without a tail wag, the evening without a companion curled at your feet. It's about finding a way to exist inside the hollow spaces while slowly rebuilding the shape of your days.

The Empty Spaces

Pets are woven into our routines in ways we often don't realize until they're gone. You wake up and instinctively glance toward the bed where they used to sleep. You reach for the leash, only to remember there's no walk today. You listen for the jingle of their tags, the sigh they gave as they settled beside you. But there is only stillness.

These missing pieces aren't just habits. They are connections. Moments of relationship and comfort. And when they're gone, life doesn't just feel sad, it feels off. You may feel unmoored. Your time structure may feel suddenly aimless. That's normal. It's not a sign of weakness; it's a sign that they mattered deeply, even in the ordinary.

When the Silence Feels Loud

One of the hardest adjustments after losing a pet is the **unfamiliar silence** that settles into the spaces they used to fill. The absence of their sounds — paws on the floor, meows for dinner, the jingle of their collar can feel deafening.

It's okay to admit that you miss the noise. That you sometimes leave the TV on just to avoid the quiet. That you still instinctively reach for the leash or open the door carefully in case they're waiting.

These phantom routines are signs of a deep connection, not weakness. In time, the silence may still ache, but it will also become a kind of quiet shrine to the love you shared.

The Loneliness of Habits

Pets are our quiet witnesses. They sit beside us through heartbreak and healing. They form the soundtrack to our solitude and the punctuation marks in our day.

When they're gone, we don't just lose a friend, we lose a pattern of being. They prompted movement: feedings, walks, outdoor breaks, belly rubs, bedtime routines. Without them, our days lose shape. Time stretches. We notice every empty pause.

You might feel the urge to fill the space immediately. Or you might want to let the emptiness be. There is no right answer. But understanding that what you're experiencing isn't just emotional, it's also behavioral — can help. Your brain and body are grieving the absence of routine, not just the pet who created it.

Building a New Routine (Gently)

Grief will disrupt your rhythms. But creating even small moments of structure can provide comfort. You don't need to overhaul your schedule; you just need a few soft anchors.

Ideas for Gentle Replacements:

- **Morning ritual:** Light a candle in their memory. Write a one-sentence journal entry about how you're feeling.
- **Walk alone:** If you walked with your pet daily, continue the walk in their honor. Take a different route if the usual one is too painful.
- **Meal moments:** If mealtime is shared, make your meals intentional. Light a small candle, play music, or sit where they used to sit.
- **End-of-day pause:** Reflect for five minutes before bed. Say goodnight to them, just as you used to.

The goal isn't to forget or to "replace." It's to soothe the aching gaps by slowly weaving a new rhythm, one that still honors the love.

Continuing the Bond in Daily Life

Your pet may be physically gone, but the relationship doesn't end. It changes. It becomes quieter, but still very real.

Ways to Keep the Connection Alive:

- **Wear something of theirs:** A tag on a chain, a custom bracelet with their name.
- **Talk to them:** Out loud, in your mind, or in a journal.
- **Keep a memory space:** A photo in a frame. Their bed is in a corner. A small shelf with their favorite toy.
- **Daily love notes:** Write one sentence a day that begins, "Today I remembered you when…"

These practices aren't about holding on too tightly. They're about continuing a bond that never really breaks.

Small Steps Toward a New Normal

In the beginning, almost everything may feel too hard. Getting out of bed. Doing dishes. Returning home to an empty house. That's not failure. That's mourning.

But with time, the ache softens. Not because you "got over it", but because your heart learned how to carry it differently.

Celebrate the small victories:

- The first time you smiled, thinking of them.
- The first walk that didn't make you cry.
- The moment you remembered a silly memory.

You're not forgetting. You're healing.

A Letter From Your Pet – I See You

Dear Human,

I see the way you still pause at my bowl. The way you look at the spot where I used to sleep. The way your heart skips when you hear a sound that used to mean me.

I want you to know: I feel it too.

I feel your missing. I feel your remembering. I feel your love in every quiet step you take without me.

You're doing better than you think. I see the ways you still carry me. In your habits. In your tears. In your laughter when you think of my quirks.

Thank you for not rushing. For letting grief be a part of our goodbye. For letting love stay.

I'm still here. Not in the same way, but in every way that matters.

Always,

Your watchful soul-mate 🐾

Reflection Prompt: The Hardest Time of Day

Ask yourself:

- What part of the day feels most difficult without them?
- What used to happen then?
- Is there something new you could try that honors them gently in that space?

"Evenings are the hardest. That's when we used to curl up on the couch. Now I sit in silence, but I light a candle beside their photo. It helps."

Worksheet: New Routines You Can Try

Old Routine	Emotion	Gentle New Option
Morning walks	Togetherness	Solo walk with music or journaling
Feeding time	Care, connection	Light a candle; say a few words
End-of-day cuddle time	Comfort, quiet presence	Read or journal in their old spot
Afternoon play session	Joy, laughter	Visit a park or play a favorite song

Start small. Even one shift can create comfort.

Small Acts of Connection You Can Carry Forward

- Say their name aloud once a day
- Share a memory with a friend
- Wear or carry something that reminds you of them
- Light a candle on hard days
- Write in a "memory journal" once a week
- Return to a favorite shared place and leave a flower or token
- Make a small donation or act of kindness in their name
- Keep their photo somewhere you'll see it often
- Talk to them when you need comfort

Grief doesn't end with a calendar; it transforms. And connection doesn't disappear, it evolves.

Closing Poem

"The Quiet Hours"

They are not here, but they are near,
In moments when the day feels long.
In habits shaped by love and time,
In places where you still belong.

You walk alone, but not unloved,
You miss the noise, the cheerful bark.
But every silence now is filled,
With pawprints pressed into your heart.

You don't have to rush into your new life. You're allowed to walk through it slowly, one step at a time, carrying the memory of your pet like a quiet companion beside you. The bond remains. And so will they, in the shape of everything your love once touched.

When Others Don't Understand: Dealing with Dismissive Reactions

One of the hardest parts of grieving a pet is not just the pain, but the loneliness of that pain. It's not always met with casseroles or sympathy cards. You might find that your grief is invisible to others, or worse, invalidated.

You may have heard:

- *"Just welcome a new one."*
- *"It was just a dog."*
- *"At least it wasn't a child or a parent."*

These phrases sting. Not just because they're careless, but because they suggest that what you're feeling is too much, as if loving a pet deeply is something to be embarrassed about.

But here's the truth: **You're not overreacting. You're not being dramatic. You're mourning a profound bond. And no one else has the right to measure that.**

Why People Don't Always Understand

Most people don't intend to hurt you. But that doesn't mean their words aren't painful. There are many reasons someone might minimize your grief:

1. They've Never Had a Deep Bond with an Animal

If someone has never truly loved a pet, they may not understand the emotional role pets play, especially as companions, healers, and emotional anchors.

2. Cultural or Generational Differences

In some cultures, or older generations, pets were viewed more as property or workers than family. That doesn't mean your grief isn't valid; it just means they were taught differently.

3. Discomfort with Grief

Some people simply don't know how to deal with grief in any form. They may deflect, downplay, or make light of your loss because it makes them uncomfortable.

4. Misplaced Attempts at Comfort

"Get another one" is often meant to help, but it skips over the essential truth that pets are not replaceable. Love is not something you just swap out.

Understanding these reasons doesn't excuse their insensitivity. But it can help you detach from taking it personally. Their limitations don't define your loss.

Scripts for Gentle Responses

Sometimes you want to speak up. Other times, you don't have the energy. Here are a few simple responses you can choose from, depending on the moment.

If You Want to Educate:

- "They were part of my family. This loss is real for me."
- "Grief doesn't depend on species. It depends on love."

If You Want to Set a Boundary:

- "I know you mean well, but that's not helpful right now."
- "I'm not looking for advice, just a little understanding."

If You Want to Exit the Conversation:

- "I'd rather not talk about this with someone who doesn't get it."
- "Thanks, but I'm going to excuse myself."

If You Want to Say Nothing:

Silence is a full sentence. You don't owe anyone an explanation for your grief.

Validating Yourself When No One Else Does

Sometimes, the hardest person to convince is yourself. When others are dismissive, you may begin to doubt your own experience.

"Maybe I'm overreacting…"

"Maybe I shouldn't be this upset…"

Pause. Breathe. Let this truth in:

Grief is not a competition. It doesn't need to be justified.

You are grieving because you loved deeply. That is not a weakness. That is sacred.

It's okay if your coworkers don't understand why you took the day off. It's okay if your neighbor changes the subject. You know the bond you shared. And that's what matters most.

Finding A Safe Space

You deserve to talk about your grief with people who understand. People who won't rush you, minimize you, or try to fix you. Seek out safe spaces — a trusted friend who knew your pet.

You don't have to explain yourself in these places. You can just be. And sometimes, that's the most healing gift of all.

If your current circle isn't offering the support you need, that's not a sign you're too much, it's a sign you need *more suitable companionship in this chapter of your life.*

Consider these alternative support options:

- **Online pet loss forums or groups**, where people truly understand the depth of this grief.
- **Local pet loss support groups** are often held by shelters or veterinary clinics.
- **Grief-trained therapists** who acknowledge pet loss as legitimate.
- **Animal chaplains or spiritual counselors** who help people through transitions with animals.

You deserve a place to speak your pet's name and have someone nod, not flinch. You deserve a space where your stories bring warmth, not awkward silence.

A Letter From Your Pet – I Saw You Try

Dear Human,

I saw you try to explain. I saw you stumble for words when someone asked, "Why are you so upset?" I saw the look on your face when they didn't understand.

It's okay. Not everyone will get it.

But I did.

I knew what we had. I felt the way your voice softened when you spoke to me. The way you laughed when I was silly. The way you curled around me when life felt hard.

That was real. That was love.

You don't have to prove our bond. It existed in every ordinary day. In every shared breath. In every quiet night.

Let them say what they want. I know the truth.

And I'm still holding it. Always.

Your proud companion 🐾

Reflection Prompt: What Hurt, What Helped

Think of a time someone responded to your grief, positively or negatively. Ask yourself:

- What did they say that hurt you?
- What do you wish they had said instead?
- What could you say to someone else who might feel this same hurt one day?

"My coworker said, 'You'll get over it.' I wish she had said, 'Tell me about them. What were they like?'"

What You Deserve to Hear (Even If Others Don't Say It)

- "I'm so sorry. I know how much they meant to you."
- "Your grief is valid. They were family."
- "You gave them a beautiful life."
- "There's no timeline for this. Take your time."
- "It's okay to cry. I'm here."

- "You don't have to explain why this hurts so much."
- "They were lucky to have you."
- "You don't have to move on. You can move with love."

If no one has said these things to you, let this chapter say them now.

You are heard. You are seen. You are not alone.

Closing Poem

"Unspoken"

They didn't see the daily ways,
You cared, you laughed, you gave.
They didn't hear the whispered names,
Or watch you try to save.

They didn't see the way you broke,
When fur was all you found.
They didn't know the sacred grief,
That doesn't make a sound.

But I know. I saw. I stayed.
And love like ours will never fade.

Not everyone will understand. But those who do, those who feel this kind of love, will never question your grief. And in the quiet spaces of your heart, where love still echoes, you don't need anyone's permission to feel your grief. You only need to know that it matters. Because it does.

Children, Families, and Pet Loss: Supporting Young Grievers

When a pet dies, it leaves a gap in the family that's often felt most profoundly by children. For many kids, a pet is their first friend, their playmate, their secret-keeper, their source of unconditional love. It may also be their first experience with death.

Helping a child navigate the loss of a pet is not just about managing their sadness. It's about shaping their understanding of grief, compassion, and emotional honesty for the rest of their lives. This chapter is here to support you in guiding them through that tender journey.

How Children Understand Death at Different Ages

Grief looks different for children depending on their age and emotional development. Here's a general guide:

Ages 2–5: The Magical Thinkers

- See death as temporary or reversible

- May ask repeatedly when the pet is coming back
- May believe their thoughts or actions caused the death (e.g., "I forgot to feed them")
- Express grief through play, clinginess, or changes in behavior

Ages 6–9: The Curious Feelers

- Begin to understand that death is final, but may still have magical thinking
- Often ask specific, even graphic questions (e.g., "What happened to their body?")
- May worry about other people or pets dying next
- Feel guilt or blame

Ages 10+: The Deep Processors

- Understand that death is irreversible and universal
- May experience grief similarly to adults: sadness, withdrawal, anger
- Often try to be "brave" or hide feelings
- May seek outlets through writing, journaling, or art

How to Talk to Children About Pet Loss

Grief is not something to shield children from. It's something to walk through with them. Honest, gentle conversation is key.

Use Clear Language

Avoid phrases like "went to sleep" or "ran away." These can create confusion or fear.

Say instead:

- "They were very sick, and their bodies stopped working."
- "We made the decision to help them die peacefully, so they didn't have to suffer."

Invite Questions

Children may ask the same question many times. That's okay. They're trying to process something enormous with a developing brain.

Be calm. Be repetitive. Be reassuring.

Share Your Emotions

Letting them see your sadness permits them to feel theirs. Say things like:

- "I miss them too."

- "It's okay to cry."
- "I'm feeling really sad today."

This creates emotional safety.

What Children Might Feel or Do

Every child is different, but here are some common reactions:

- Crying or emotional outbursts
- Quietness or withdrawal
- Guilt ("Did I do something wrong?")
- Regression (thumb-sucking, bedwetting)
- Sleep difficulties or nightmares
- Wanting to get another pet immediately
- Reenacting the death in play or drawings

Let them grieve in their own way. There's no "right" response. Just be present, patient, and validating.

How to Support Children Through the Grief

1. Reassure Them

- "This is not your fault."
- "You gave them a great life."
- "They loved you so much."

2. Include Them in the Goodbye

Let them:

- Say goodbye in their own words
- Write a letter or draw a picture
- Place a toy or flower in the pet's resting place

3. Encourage Expression

- Drawing pictures of their pet
- Writing or telling stories about them
- Creating a photo album or scrapbook together
- Talking about favorite memories

4. Normalize Grief

Say things like:

- "It's normal to feel sad, mad, or confused."

- "Some days are harder than others."
- "You don't have to stop missing them."

Grieving as a Family

When a pet dies, the whole family is affected, but not always in the same way. Grieving together as a family isn't always synchronized.

One child might cry openly for weeks. Another might seem unaffected, detached. Parents might hold back their own tears to stay "strong," while a teenager might retreat into silence.

These differences don't mean anyone is grieving *wrong*, they just reveal the many shapes grief takes. Encourage every family member to grieve in their own way, at their own pace.

Children notice these differences and take cues from them. It's okay to grieve differently, but it's helpful to:

- Talk openly as a family
- Validate each other's feelings
- Share stories and memories together

You might create gentle, shared rituals that give space for each person:

- A weekly "memory circle" where everyone shares a story about the pet
- Lighting a candle before dinner
- Creating art together (drawings, collages, memory jars)
- Naming a star after the pet and looking for it together at night

Family Memory Ideas:

- Create a "Pet Memory Box" with drawings, toys, or letters
- Make a family photo album
- Designate a shelf or spot in the house for remembrance

By anchoring grief in togetherness, you show children (and yourself) that no one is alone in this sadness. These rituals give children a sense of inclusion and structure. They remind everyone that the pet mattered, and still does.

The Long-Term Impact on Young Hearts

Children don't always have the language for big feelings, but they *remember* how they were supported. The way you respond to a pet's passing helps shape how they'll handle future losses.

You're teaching them that it's okay to cry. That love is worth the risk of grief. That saying goodbye doesn't mean forgetting.

Sometimes, older children or teens may act like they "don't care." But even aloofness is a form of protection. Try saying, *"I know this might be hard to talk about, but I'm here when you're ready."* That leaves the door open without pressure.

Years from now, your child may look back and realize: *That pet was my first best friend. And when they died, I learned how to hold space for loss — with love instead of fear.*

A Letter From the Pet – For Young Hearts

Dear Little Human,

I saw your tears. I felt your hugs. I loved every game we played and every time you sneaked me extra treats.

I didn't want to go. But I want you to know: I wasn't scared. I wasn't alone. I felt your love all around me.

Now I run fast again. I don't hurt anymore. I chase butterflies and roll in the sunshine.

When you miss me, close your eyes. I'm right there in your memories. I'm in your laugh. I'm in your heart.

You were my best friend.

And I will love you forever.

Your forever buddy 🐾

Prompt for Parents: Noticing Your Child's Grief

- What have you noticed in your child's behavior or mood since the loss?
- How have they expressed sadness or confusion?
- What seemed to bring them comfort?
- What conversations helped? What was difficult?

Write it down, or simply reflect. Every child's grief is a clue to how they understand love.

Activity Ideas for Families

- **Draw Their Favorite Memory:** Use crayons, markers, or paint
- **Write a Story About Their Life:** "Once upon a time, there was a dog named Max who loved to…"
- **Plant Something Together:** A flower, bush, or tree in the pet's memory
- **Create a Memory Jar:** Decorate a jar and fill it with memories on slips of paper

- **Make a Stuffed Animal or Pillow:** Use an old toy, T-shirt, or blanket

These activities help children feel connected and give grief a way to move gently through the body.

What to Say, and What to Avoid

Helpful Things to Say:

- "I know you loved them a lot."
- "It's okay to be sad."
- "Do you want to talk about them?"
- "They were lucky to have you."
- "Let's remember them together."

Avoid Saying:

- "They went to sleep." (confusing or scary)
- "Don't cry."
- "We'll just get a new one."
- "You're being too sensitive."
- "You're too young to understand."

Kids do understand. Maybe not with words, but with their hearts.

Closing Poem

"Little Hands, Big Love"

You brushed my fur with tiny hands,
And fed me snacks I didn't need.
You whispered secrets only I heard,
And followed me with joyful speed.

You made me feel like I was magic,
A knight, a prince, a silly clown.
And when I hurt, you kissed my nose,
And sat with me when I lay down.

I may be gone, but not from you,
You carry me in all you do.
Your love was real, your heart was kind,
You were my human. I was yours. We were perfectly aligned.

Children are resilient. But they're also deeply sensitive. When we take the time to honor their grief, we teach them the value of love and how to carry it forward, even when the one they loved has gone. That's not just healing. That's legacy.

Healing Through Helping: Finding Meaning After Loss

There comes a moment in the grief journey — not right away, not all at once — when the heaviness begins to shift. Not disappear, but shift. You might wake up one day and think of your pet with more warmth than ache. You might feel the urge to do something with all that love still buzzing in your heart.

This chapter is about that moment. The moment you realize:

I want their life to mean something beyond the goodbye.

Helping doesn't mean rushing. It doesn't mean trying to erase the pain. Helping is simply this: letting your grief take shape in love. **In action. In something new.**

The Role of Meaning in Healing

Grief can leave us feeling powerless. It breaks routines, overwhelms emotions, and sometimes makes life feel hollow. But purpose can be a lantern in the dark.

When we channel our pain into purpose, it gives us:

- A sense of control
- A reason to get out of bed
- A way to honor the bond we had

You don't have to change the world. You only have to respond to this truth:

Love never ends — it only changes form.

Helping Others as a Path to Connection

Grief often leaves us feeling powerless. Something vital was taken from us, and we couldn't stop it. But helping others, especially animals or fellow grievers can be a way to *reclaim agency*.

When you feel ready, consider ways to extend your love outward. Not as a replacement, but as a tribute.

This doesn't have to be dramatic. You don't need to start a nonprofit or run a marathon in your pet's name. Sometimes healing comes through the **quietest forms of service:**

1. Volunteer at a Shelter or Rescue

Animals in shelters need affection, care, and time. Spending an hour a week walking dogs, cleaning kennels, or simply sitting with scared cats can be a powerful act of healing.

Many grieving pet parents say, "I went in thinking I was helping them, but they helped me."

2. Donate in Your Pet's Name

Consider donating to:

- Animal shelters
- Wildlife rescue centers
- Pet hospice programs
- Veterinary research or care assistance funds

Even a small donation can feel like a meaningful gesture. Some people choose to do this on birthdays or adoption anniversaries.

3. Foster a Pet When Ready

Fostering isn't a replacement. It's a way to offer temporary safety and love. Some people find fostering to be a low-pressure way to reconnect with animals while grieving.

4. Support Other Grieving Pet Owners

You've walked this road. You know how isolating it can be. Reaching out to others can create shared strength:

- Join or lead a pet loss support group
- Write letters or cards to others in mourning
- Comment on online forums or social media posts with compassion

Every small act whispers: My love still matters. And it can still do good. You become a voice of comfort, just by saying: "Me too. I get it."

Creative Acts of Legacy

Your pet's life can inspire beauty, expression, and even change. Let your love take creative shape.

Ways to Create a Living Legacy:

- **Start a Pet Memorial Blog or Page:** Share stories, photos, and lessons your pet taught you
- **Write a Letter Series or Booklet:** "Letters to My Pet" can become a beautiful tribute
- **Make Art:** Paint their portrait, create a collage, or design a digital memory album

- **Sponsor a Shelter Kennel:** Place a plaque with your pet's name
- **Launch a Micro-Project:** Create a "Pet Grief Comfort Kit" to give friends or shelters

Whatever you make doesn't need to be perfect—it only needs to be honest.

Letting Your Pet's Values Live On

Each pet brings a certain energy to our lives. Some were playful. Some were fiercely loyal. Others had a calming, almost spiritual presence.

Ask yourself: **What did my pet teach me? What kind of energy did they leave behind?**

Now ask: **Where can I bring that energy into the world?**

- If your pet was a goofball, bring laughter to someone else's day.
- If they were nurturing, offer comfort to another grieving person.
- If they were brave, take a leap you've been putting off.

By becoming a living reflection of what they gave you, you keep them close, not in sadness, but in strength.

Helping Yourself Is Helping Too!

Let's be clear: you don't have to help others to grieve correctly. Sometimes, the most healing thing you can do is tend to your own heart.

Self-care is service.

- Sleeping more
- Taking daily walks again
- Drinking enough water
- Seeing a therapist
- Making your bed with care

These aren't small. They're sacred. They say: **I still matter. I'm still here.**

Helping yourself is the foundation. From there, you'll know when you're ready to help others.

A Letter From Your Pet – The Love You Carry

Dear Human,

You've taken care of me so well. And now, you're learning to take care of others—and yourself—with the same kindness.

Every time you help another being, you carry a piece of me with you. Every time you extend a hand, you're extending our story. You are showing the world what love looks like after goodbye.

I don't need a statue or a big memorial. You've already honored me by being the kind of person who loved me so deeply, and continues to love out loud.

You don't have to do anything grand. Just live with softness. Keep choosing love. That's enough.

And if you ever doubt your impact, just look at how I turned out.

Proud of you always,

Your forever sidekick 🐾

Reflection Prompt: One Small Act of Meaning

Ask yourself:

- What's one small thing I could do this week in their honor?
- Is there someone, human or animal, I could show kindness to?
- What would my pet smile about if they saw me do it?

"I donated a blanket to the local shelter. It felt right—my dog loved cozy things. It made me smile through the tears."

Ways to Help and Heal (Solo + Community)

Type of Action	Solo Option	Community Option
Emotional Support	Journal your grief journey	Join a pet loss group
Physical Acts of Care	Light a candle daily for them	Volunteer at a rescue shelter

Creative Legacy	Create a tribute scrapbook	Start a memorial page or blog
Charitable Giving	Donate food/supplies to a local org	Fundraise or host a donation drive
Supporting Others	Send a card to a grieving friend	Start a peer-support message thread

How to Know You're Ready to Help Again

- I think of my pet and feel more warmth than pain
- I have a desire to give, not to distract
- I feel emotionally steady most days
- Helping feels like a choice, not a burden
- I'm okay with taking breaks or saying no
- I want others to feel less alone

Even if only a few of these are true, that's enough to begin. And if none are yet, that's okay too. You'll know when it's time.

Closing Poem

"In the Doing"

I searched for you in quiet skies,
In tears, in photos, in old toys.
But then I found you in a smile,
Shared with a dog who needed joy.

I gave a blanket. Brought a treat.
Held a paw with trembling grace.
And felt, in all the giving back,
Your steady heartbeat in its place.

Helping after a loss isn't about fixing anything. It's about tending to what still lives — the love, the kindness, the connection. When you give, you carry your pet forward. Not as a memory only, but as a presence reshaped into compassion.

And that? That's the kind of forever love that never fades.

Opening Your Heart Again: Welcoming a New Pet Companion

There's a quiet moment that comes after grief begins to soften. You catch yourself smiling at a memory instead of crying. You notice the silence in the house, but it doesn't sting the same way. And then, sometimes unexpectedly, the thought appears: Should I get another pet?

It's a fragile thought, full of hope and hesitation. You may immediately feel guilty for even considering it. Or maybe it brings you relief, something to look forward to. Both reactions are valid.

This chapter is about gently exploring that question. Not to push you, not to decide for you, but to walk alongside you as you ask: What does love look like now?

The Complexity of Loving Again

You loved your pet deeply. That kind of love doesn't vanish. So, of course, the idea of welcoming another can feel complicated. You might worry:

- "Will this mean I've moved on?"
- "What if I don't feel the same connection?"
- "Am I just trying to fill the emptiness?"
- "Would my pet feel replaced?"

Let this truth land softly: **love isn't limited.** Your heart is not a shelf that holds only one beloved at a time. It's more like a garden. Love given and received enriches the soil, and from that, more love can grow.

Grief and new love can coexist. One doesn't erase the other. The depth of your grief often reflects the depth of your capacity to love again.

The Guilt of Moving Forward

For many grieving pet parents, the thought of bringing another animal into their lives feels almost like betrayal. *If I loved them so much, how can I even think about another pet?* That question sits heavily on the heart.

But here's a truth worth repeating: **welcoming a new companion does not mean replacing the one you lost.** It means that your love was so strong, so life-affirming, that it still has more to give.

Love isn't a limited resource. It expands. You can carry the memory of one pet while making space for another. The guilt you feel is love, trying to find a new way to express itself. Let it soften over time.

Guilt vs. Readiness

Guilt is a natural response, but it doesn't mean you're doing something wrong. It means your heart is still full of love for the one who's gone.

Readiness doesn't mean forgetting. It means you feel stable enough to begin a new chapter, one that honors the past without being bound by it.

Ask yourself:

- Am I looking for a new companion to heal, not to replace?
- Does the idea bring comfort, not just escape?
- Can I hold space for a new personality, not just old habits?

If you're not sure, give it time. This is not a race. There is no finish line.

What to Consider Before Bringing a New Pet Home

It's tempting to want to "fix the silence" right away. But welcoming a new animal is a big step. Here are a few things to gently reflect on:

1. Emotional Readiness

- Are you still overwhelmed by grief every day?
- Can you imagine forming a new bond, even if it feels different?
- Can I think about my late pet with more warmth than pain?

2. Practical Considerations

- Are you financially, physically, and mentally prepared?
- Do you have time, space, and support?
- Do I have the emotional and physical energy for another companion?

3. Motivation Check

- Are you adopting out of loneliness, guilt, or genuine desire to give love again?

- Do I want to honor my pet's legacy by giving love to another animal in need?

If the idea brings guilt or sadness, give yourself more time. If it brings curiosity, warmth, or hope, follow that thread.

There's no shame in any answer. Just awareness.

Choosing the Right Pet (and Letting Go of Comparison)

No two pets are alike. Just like no two friendships or loves are alike. It's natural to want to find a pet who reminds you of the one you lost, but try to leave space for surprise.

Let the new animal be who they are.

They may be goofier. Quieter. More distant or more cuddly. This doesn't mean the bond will be less, it will simply be different. And different can still be beautiful.

Some people feel an instant connection. Others grow into it slowly. Either is okay.

Remember: **you're not replacing — you're expanding.**

You Can Say No, or Not Yet

There's no right time to adopt again. For some, it's a few weeks. For others, a few years. You might never want to adopt again, and that's okay, too. The only timeline that matters is yours.

Opening your heart again isn't required. It's just an option.

You might decide that your pet was your one great companion, and that's enough. You might decide to foster occasionally. You might volunteer instead. You might adopt many years later.

There is no timeline. There is no rule. There is only your truth.

A Letter From Your Pet – If You Love Again

Dear Human,

I've watched you grieve. I've felt every tear you cried for me. And now, I see you wonder: Is it okay to love again?

Yes. A thousand times, yes.

If you open your home again, it doesn't take anything away from me. It adds to the love I left behind.

You see, I want your heart to stay open. Because your heart made my life so full. Why wouldn't I want another soul to feel that same joy?

They won't be me. And that's okay. They'll be someone new. But you'll love them with the same beautiful spirit you gave to me.

Don't rush. There's no pressure. Just know: if you choose to love again, you have my full blessing.

Forever grateful,

Your first fur-angel 🐾

Reflection Prompt: What Would They Say?

Take five quiet minutes. Ask yourself:

- If my pet could talk to me about loving again, what would they say?
- What fears am I holding onto?
- What possibilities excite me?
- If I never got another pet, how would I still honor their memory?

"I think he'd nudge me toward it. Not right now, but eventually. He always liked having other dogs around."

A Gentle Nudge – From the Pet Who Still Loves You

Dear Human,

I see you looking at shelters online, then closing the tab. I see the way your heart leaps when you pass a dog at the park, then sinks in your chest a moment later. It's okay. You don't have to rush.

But let me say this: If another soul walks into your life one day, I won't feel replaced. I'll feel proud.

Because you taught me how to trust. You showed me what love looks like. And if another animal gets to experience that… what a beautiful legacy we built together.

I'll always be your first in some way. Your once-in-a-lifetime, maybe. But there's more love in you yet.

Love you always,

Your silent cheerleader, paws in the sky 🐾

Reflection Prompt: Am I Ready?

Try journaling with these questions in mind:

- What kind of relationship do I hope to have with a future pet?
- What lessons did my last companion teach me that I want to carry forward?
- What emotions come up when I imagine adopting again — joy, fear, guilt, hope?
- What do I need to forgive in myself before I'm ready to love again?

Am I Ready? (A Gentle Self-Check)

- I think of my pet and feel gratitude more often than pain
- I miss having a pet — not just them, but the companionship itself
- I have space in my life, home, and heart
- I understand this new pet will be different, and that's okay

- I feel emotionally steady enough for new routines and responsibilities
- I want to give love, not fill a void

You don't need to check all the boxes. Even one or two might mean you're nearing readiness. If none feel true yet, trust that your heart is still healing, and that's okay.

Closing Poem

"A Door That Never Closes"

You were my first hello,
My softest sigh at night.
You walked beside my shadow,
You were my guiding light.

Now silence fills the hallway,
Your bowl sits tucked away.
And still, I feel you near me,
In every gentle day.

Another may come someday,
With paws and eyes brand new.
Not to replace or cover,
But to remind me, I can love like you.

Love never asks us to choose. It simply asks us to expand. If and when you open your heart again, do it in your time, in your way. Whether that day comes soon or not at all, know this: the love you shared will always be enough.

And it will always be with you.

A Final Note: The Shape of Love After Loss

Grief doesn't end; it evolves. It weaves itself into the fabric of your days in quieter ways. Over time, what once brought only tears begins to bring warmth. A memory. A smile. A breath that doesn't collapse.

You may find yourself saying their name out loud just to hear it again. That's not regression, it's reverence. You're allowing love to echo. And that echo is healing.

If you're wondering whether you'll ever be the same again, the answer is: you won't. **But you'll be something new.** Someone who has loved deeply, lost dearly, and still chooses to live with tenderness. That is not a wound. That is a strength.

By now, you've walked through sorrow, memory, anger, comfort, and everything in between. You've sat with the stillness, and maybe even smiled through the tears. You've honored your pet's life, faced the weight of their absence, and taken small, brave steps toward healing.

Some people worry that healing means letting go, or that moving forward means moving on. But that's not true. Healing simply means you've made space for the love to live beside the loss. That you can remember without falling apart. That you can carry their memory as a blessing, not just a burden.

Your pet wouldn't want you to stay in the ache. They'd want you to carry their joy forward. In your kindness. In your laughter. In your next brave act of love.

If it still hurts, that's okay. If you still cry, that's okay. If some days feel heavier than others, that's okay too. Grief doesn't ask for timelines, it asks for space. For gentleness. For honesty.

Your love didn't end when your pet died. It changed shape. It's in how you speak about them. In how you remember. In the way you care more deeply now, perhaps, for other animals or people. It's in every kind gesture you give, every bit of empathy you show, and every heartbeat you carry forward.

Some readers may go on to open their hearts again to a new companion. Others may choose to cherish the love they had as a once-in-a-lifetime experience. Both paths are valid.

Both are beautiful. Only you know what feels true to your journey.

No matter where this book finds you in your grief, I hope it reminds you of something vital: you are not alone.

You loved well. You gave your heart. And you are still giving, even now.

Thank you for letting me walk with you through these pages. May your memories bring warmth. May your healing come gently. And may you always feel your pet's love, woven into your life in ways seen and unseen.

With quiet strength and love,

— *Elara Sage*

One Last Letter

Dear Human,

By now, I hope you've seen how much love you gave me. I hope you've remembered the games we played, the sleepy afternoons, the silly things I did to make you laugh. I hope you've stopped blaming yourself for things you couldn't control.

You were everything to me. And I know you still carry me in your heart.

One day, you might open your heart to another companion, and that won't replace me. It will honor me. Because love like ours doesn't disappear. It grows. It opens doors.

Until then, I'll be watching, in the rustle of trees, in the quiet moonlight, in the warmth of memories you hold tight.

I'm okay. I hope you are, too.

With unending love,

Your forever friend 🐾

Bonus Content

Pet Memory Pages

Use these pages to reflect, remember, and reconnect with the life you shared. There is no right or wrong way to fill them in—only your truth.

My Pet's Name:

Nickname(s):

Type/Breed:

How We Met:

Years Together:

Favorite Memory Together:

....

....

....

....

....

....

....

....

....

....

Something Funny They Always Did:

....

....

....

....

....

....

....

....

Favorite Toy or Treat:

....

....

....

....

....

....

....

....

What I Miss the Most:

....

....

....

....

....

....

....

....

What They Taught Me:

....

....

....

....

....

....

....

One Last Thing I Wish I Could Say:

....

....

....

....

....

....

....

Journal Prompts for Grieving Hearts

These prompts are here for you to write through grief, not to solve it, but to meet it honestly.

- What emotion surprised me most during this loss?
- How has my daily life changed since they passed?
- When do I feel closest to my pet now?
- What would my pet say if they saw me today?
- What moments of peace have I found in the middle of grief?
- What does healing mean to me, right now, not in the future?
- What is something small I could do to honor them this week?

Take your time. Let the pen move. Let your heart speak.

....

....

....

....

....

....

....

....

....

....

....

....

....

....

....

Letters to and from…

Writing a letter can bring clarity, comfort, and closure. Use these pages however you need.

A Letter *To* My Pet

Dear .... [Pet's Name],

....

....

....

....

....

....

....

....

....

....

....

....

....

....

....

Love always,

.... [Your Name]

Imagine a Letter *From* Your Pet

Dear .... [Your Name],

....

....

....

....

....

....

....

....

....

....

....

....

....

....

....

....

....

....

....

....

Forever yours,

.... 🐾 [Pet's Name]

Poems for the Journey

The Quiet Spot by the Door

I still expect your greeting there,
Tail tapping gently on the floor.
But silence waits where love once stood,
A quiet spot by the door.

I walk past slowly, my chest pulled tight,
Still listening for your sound.
Yet in the hush, I hear your heart —
It beats in me, all around.

Still With Me

You are the softness in my day,
The breeze that lifts the leaves.
You're in the pause before I sleep,
And in the breath that grief still heaves.

Though paws no longer tap the tile,
And toys lie still and worn —
You live in how I now love more,
In how my soul has grown.

Pet Memorial Checklist

Here are gentle ways to create a lasting tribute to your beloved companion.

- Create a framed photo collage or scrapbook
- Make a "memory shelf" with their collar, tag, or toy
- Plant a tree, flower, or garden in their honor
- Light a candle on their adoption or first day
- Write and read a eulogy or goodbye letter
- Get a custom keepsake (portrait, ornament, necklace, paw print)
- Make a donation to a shelter or animal cause in their name
- Volunteer with a rescue or foster organization

Even one of these acts can bring comfort and connection.

Grief Resources and Helplines

You're not alone. If you're struggling, please reach out. Here are some trusted options to support you:

Counseling & Support

- Lap of Love Pet Loss Resource Center: lapoflove.com/pet-loss-support
- Pet Loss Support Hotline (ASPCA): 1-877-GRIEF-10
- The Rainbow Bridge Pet Loss Grief Center: rainbowbridge.com
- The Association for Pet Loss and Bereavement (APLB): aplb.org

Books & Articles

- The Loss of a Pet by Wallace Sife
- Goodbye, Friend by Gary Kowalski
- Going Home by Jon Katz

Online Communities

- Reddit: r/petloss
- Facebook: Pet Loss Support Group
- Grieving forums hosted by animal shelters and veterinary schools

You deserve support. Reach out. Connect. Heal.

Final Words

Grief is not a problem to solve. It's a love story that doesn't end. These pages are yours now. Fill them slowly or all at once. Come back to them when you need to. They're not homework — they're healing.

And your love? Still here. Always here.

Epilogue

If you're reading these final words, take a deep breath and know this: I am profoundly proud of you.

Simply by finishing this book, you have done the most courageous thing a grieving heart can do, you have chosen to lean into your pain, to explore it, and to actively process your grief. This is not a common path.

In fact, many people who experience this kind of loss become stuck, unable to give themselves permission to move forward. You are among the brave ones who have done the difficult work, and it shows.

Moving Forward is Not Forgetting

You may feel a slight tremor of guilt right now, a fear that "moving on" means abandoning the memory of your beloved companion. Let me assure you, the opposite is true.

Moving on is not forgetting; it is remembering without crippling pain.

The truth is, your pet, the one whose life you so cherished, wouldn't want your love for them to become a barrier to your own joy. They live on not in your tears, but in the lessons you learned, the compassion you gained, and the enduring warmth they left behind.

The final phase of love is acceptance. You have honored their life by allowing yourself to grieve fully, and now, it is time to honor their legacy by allowing yourself to live fully. Your heart may never be the same size, because a piece of it now belongs to them, but the space they created can be filled with hope and light.

Your grief journey has prepared you for the future. You are stronger, more resilient, and more empathetic than you were before. Take that strength and carry it forward. Embrace the future, because your pet's love is **Still With You**.

Go gently. Go bravely. Go live a beautiful life.

— Elara Sage

The Author

Elara Sage is a writer, compassionate listener, and devoted pet parent whose work is fueled by a profound understanding of the human-animal bond. Like many readers of *Still With Me: Healing After Loss of a Pet,* she has personally experienced the depth of sorrow that comes with saying goodbye to a soulmate pet.

Her journey through grief was the catalyst for this book. Recognizing that the loss of a beloved pet is often minimized by society, Elara became committed to creating the resource she desperately searched for: a guide that validates the tears, normalizes the pain, and provides a gentle, structured path toward finding peace.

When she is not writing, Elara cherishes quiet time, often spent walking in nature and carrying forward the lessons of unconditional love taught to her by her most cherished companions. She hopes this book serves as your comforting hand, helping you remember that the joy and connection you felt are still with you.

www.ingramcontent.com/pod-product-compliance
Lightning Source LLC
Chambersburg PA
CBHW050018170726
48282CB00025B/447
* 9 7 8 8 1 9 9 2 8 2 6 6 7 *